The Piano Compendium

A Selection of Pieces for Piano

Book 1
Grades 1-3

KONSTANTINOS PAPATHEODOROU

Erebus Society

First published in Great Britain in 2017
Erebus Society

First Edition

Arrangement © Konstantinos Papatheodorou 2017

ISBN 978-1-912461-04-2

TABLE OF CONTENTS

GRADE 1

Christian Gottlob Neefe – Scherzo 3

Georg Philipp Telemann – Fantasia in G Minor 4

Giuseppe Verdi - Verdi La donna è mobile (The woman is fickle) 5

Johan Sebastian Bach – Aria in F major, BWV Anh 131 6

Joseph Haydn – Farewell Symphony in F # Minor 7

Leopold Mozart - Minuet in F Major 8

Ludwig Van Beethoven – Russian Air, Op. 107 No. 3 9

Samuel Arnold - Giga Op. 12 No. 2 Lesson in C, 3rd movt 10

Wolfgang Amadeus Mozart – Minuet in F Major 11

GRADE 2

Christian Friedrich Schale – Minuet in C Major 15

Domenico Scarlatti - Sonata in C Minor, menuetto, K. 73, L. 217 16

George Frideric Handel – Impertinence, HWB 494 17

Johann Baptist Wanhal – Cantabile, First movement from Sonatina No. 4 in G, W. XIII:125 18

Leopold Mozart – Minuet in C Major 19

Leopold Mozart – Minuet in C Major No. 2 20

Leopold Mozart – Polonaise in D Major 21

Leopold Mozart – Schwabentanz 22

Ludwig Van Beethoven – Ecossaise in G Major 23

Thomas Attwood - Allegretto 1st movement from Sonatina No. 3 in F Major.............24

Thomas Attwood - Adante 2nd movement from Sonatina No. 3 in F Major................25

Thomas Attwood - Allegretto 1st movement from Sonatina No. 1 in G Major.............26

GRADE 3

George Frideric Handel – Sonatina in G Major HWV 582 29

Johann Sebastian Bach – Bourrée in G Major BWV 1009 30

Johann Sebastian Bach – Minuet in G Major 32

Leopold Mozart – Burlesque in G Major 33

Leopold Mozart – Fantasia in F Major 34

Leopold Mozart – Musette in C Major 35

Ludwig Van Beethoven – Sonatina in G Major, Anh.5 No. 1 36

Ludwig Van Beethoven – Sonatina in F Major, Anh.5 No. 2 38

Muzio Clementi - Sonatine Op. 36 No.1 42

Muzio Clementi - Sonatine Op. 36 No.1, 3 44

GRADE 1

Scherzo

Christian Gottlob Neefe

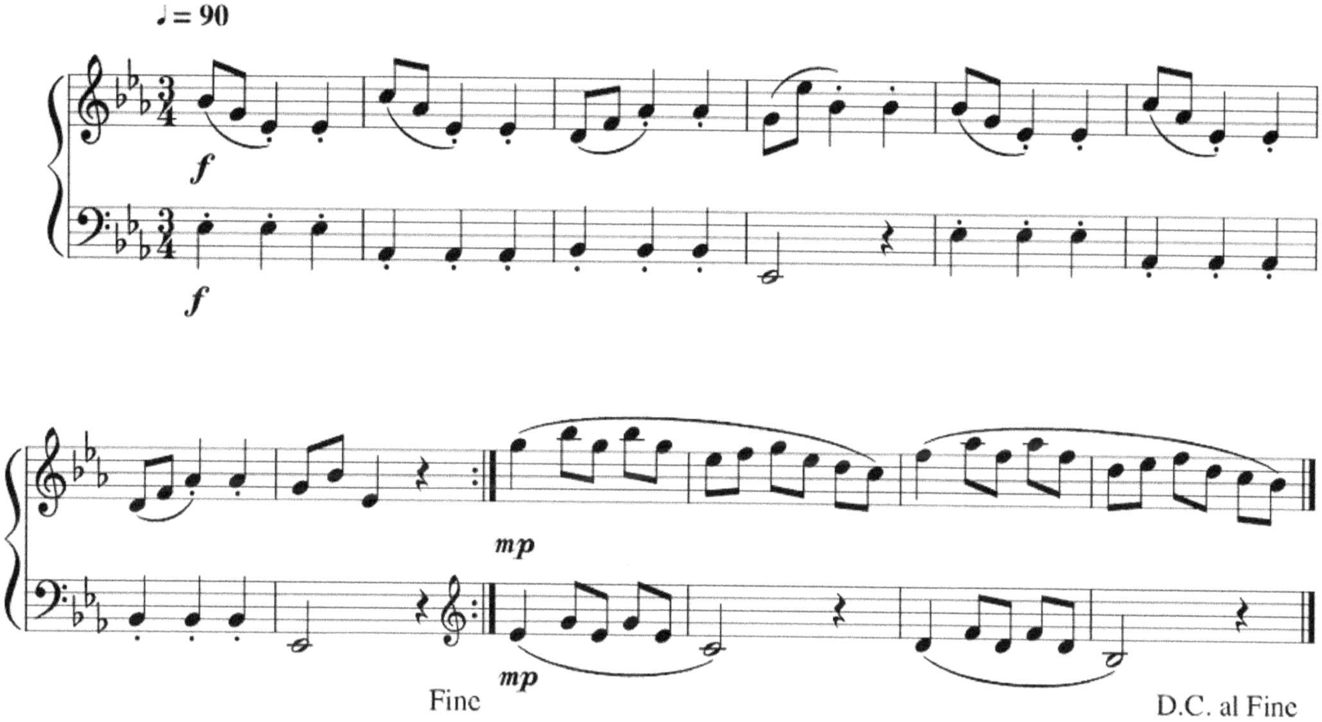

Fantasia in G Minor

TWV 33:17

Georg Philipp Telemann

Allegro Moderato

La Donna è Mobile

(The woman is fickle) from Rigoletto

Giuseppe Verdi

Aria in F major
BWV Anh 131

Johan Sebastian Bach

Farewell Symphony
Symphony 45 in F# Minor

Joseph Haydn

Minuet in F Major

Leopold Mozart

Russian Air
Op. 107 No. 3

Ludwig Van Beethoven

Giga

Op. 12 No. 2 Lesson in C, 3rd movt.

Samuel Arnold

Minuet in F Major

Wolfgang Amadeus Mozart

GRADE 2

Minuet in C Major

Christian Friedrich Schale

Sonata in C Minor
Menuetto, K. 73, L. 217

Domenico Scarlatti

Impertinence

HWB 494

George Frideric Handel

Cantabile

First movement from Sonatina No. 4 in G, W. XIII:125

Johann Baptist Wanhal

Minuet in C Major

Leopold Mozart

Minuet in C Major

No 2

Leopold Mozart

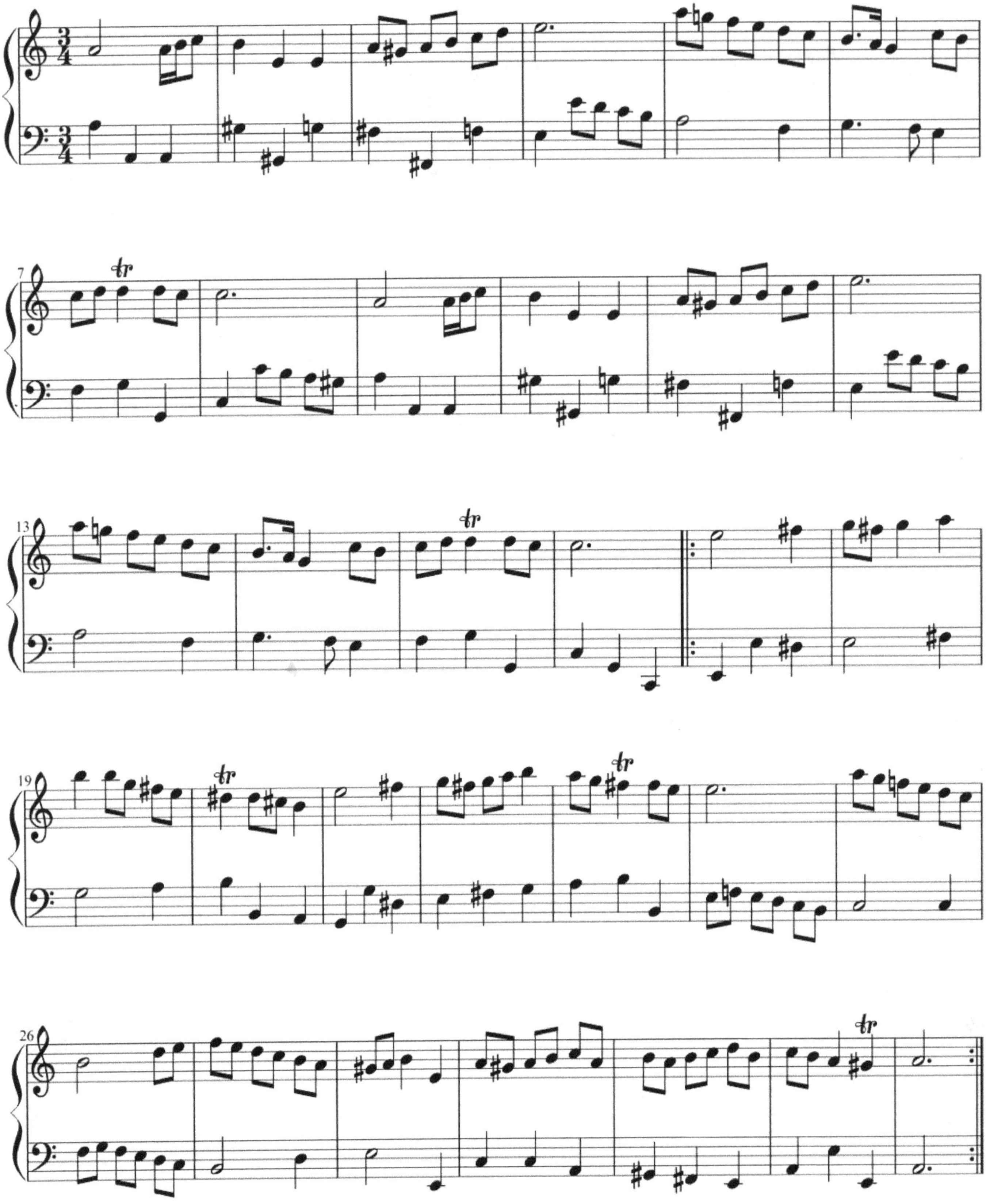

Polonaise in D Major

Leopold Mozart

Schwabentanz

Leopold Mozart

Ecossaise in G Major

Ludwig Van Beethoven

Allegretto 1st movement
from Sonatina No. 3 in F Major

Thomas Attwood

4

Adante 2nd movement
from Sonatina No. 3 in F Major

Thomas Attwood

Andante (♩ = 88)

Allegretto 1st movement
from Sonatina No. 1 in G Major

Thomas Attwood

GRADE 3

Sonatina in G Major

HWV 582

George Frideric Handel

Bourrée
in G Major BWV 1009

Johann Sebastian Bach

31

Minuet in G Major

Johann Sebastian Bach

Burlesque in G Major

Leopold Mozart

Fantasia in F Major

Leopold Mozart

Musette in C Major

Leopold Mozart

Sonatina in G Major

Anh.5 No. 1

Ludwig Van Beethoven

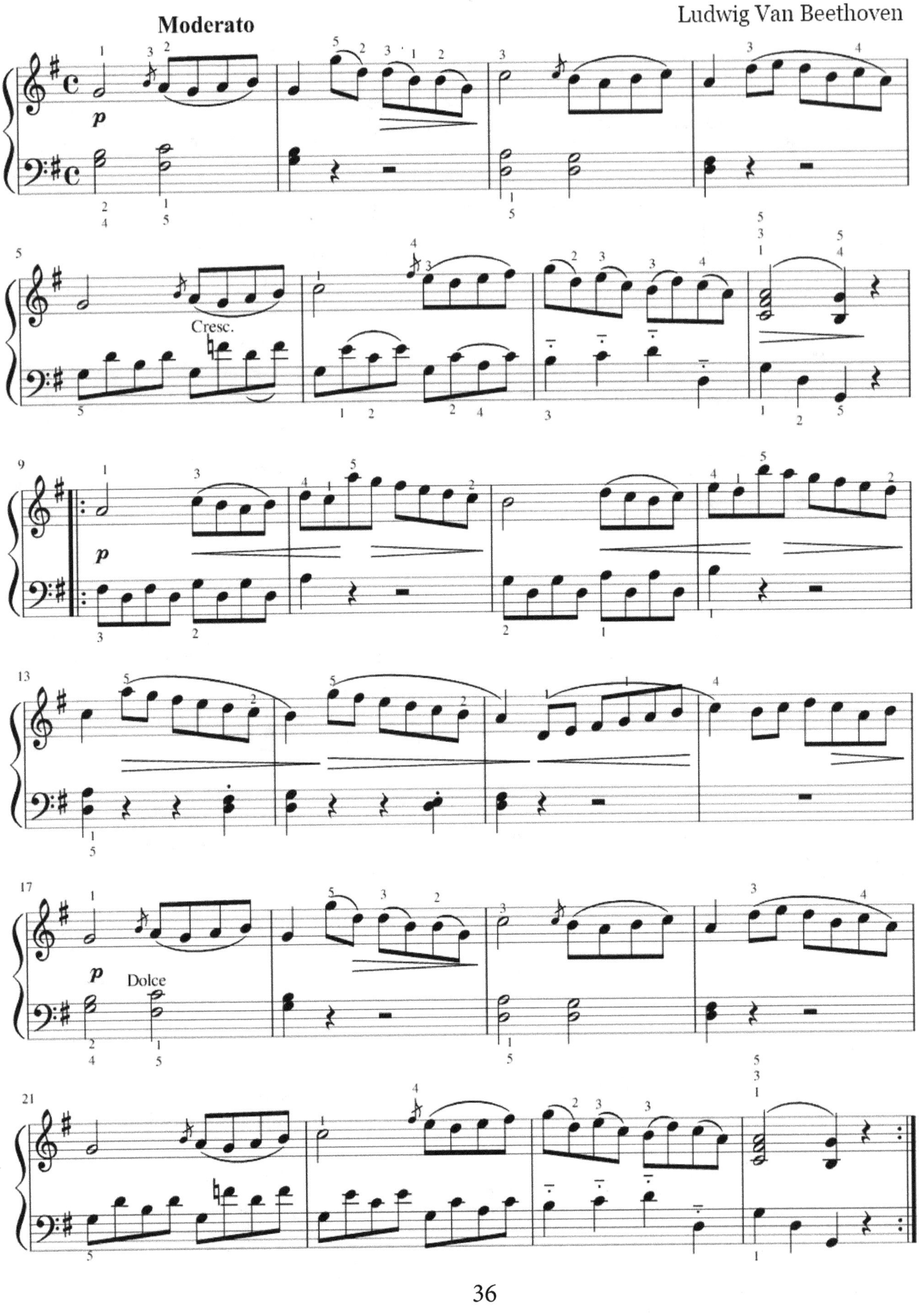

Cont.

Sonatina in F Major

Anh.5 No. 2

Ludwig Van Beethoven

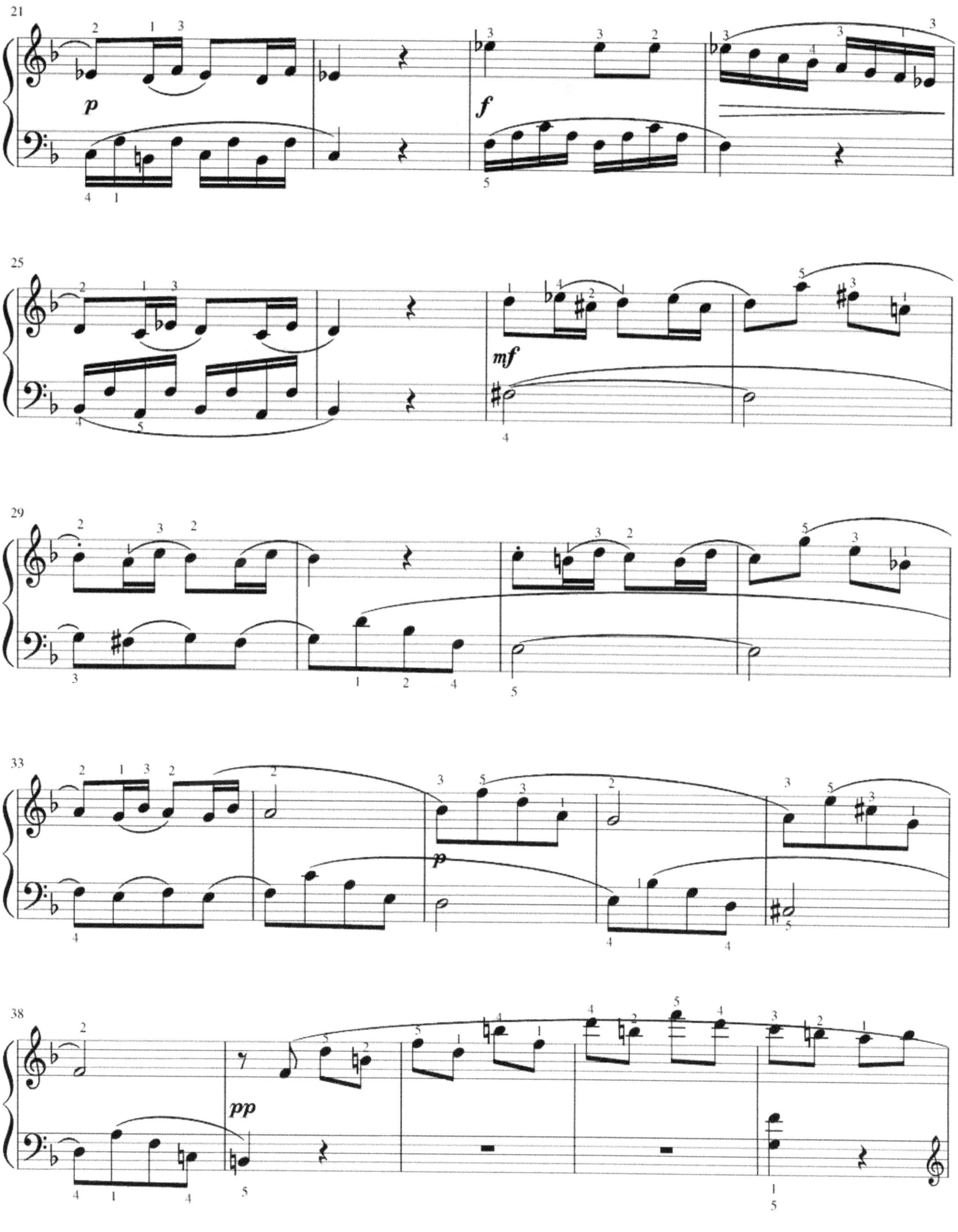
21
p
f
25
mf
29
33
p
38
pp

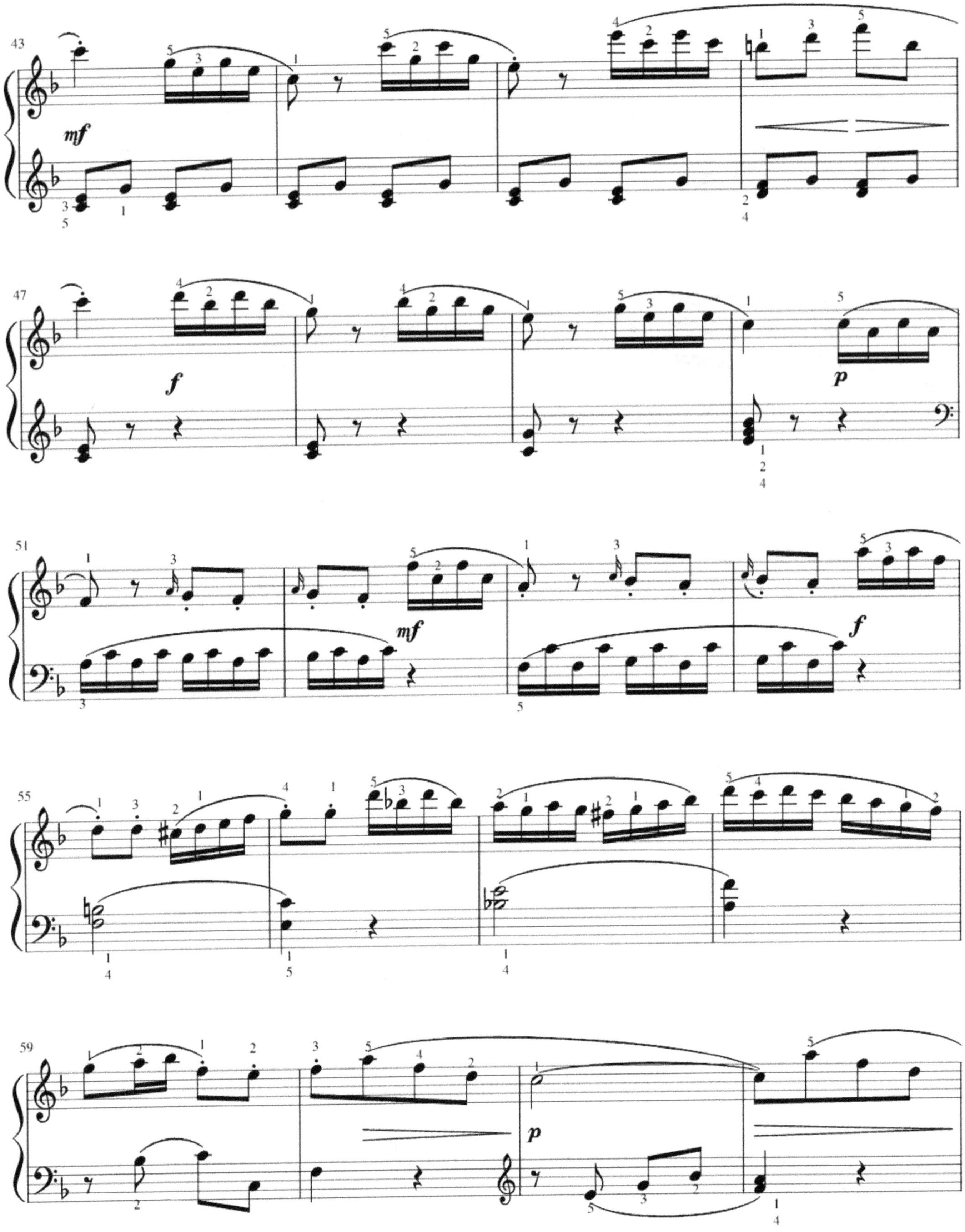

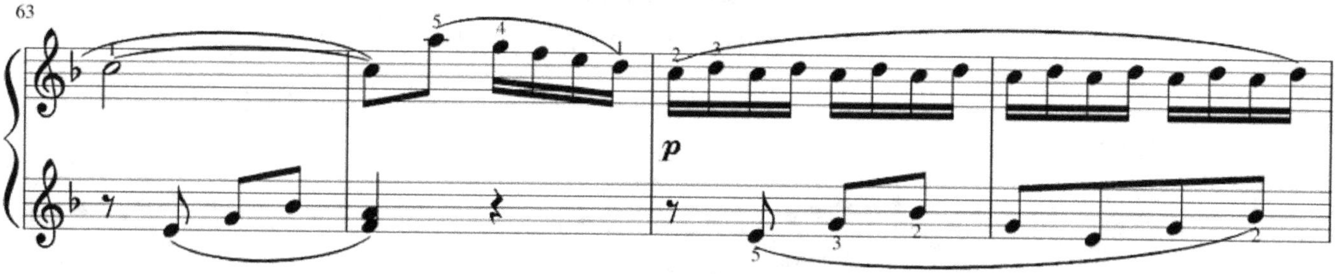
63
p
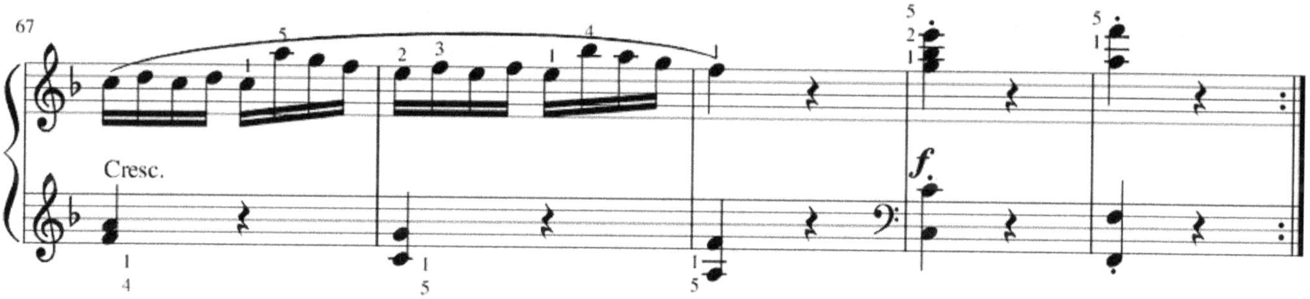
67
Cresc.
f

Sonatine

Op. 36 No.1

Muzio Clementi

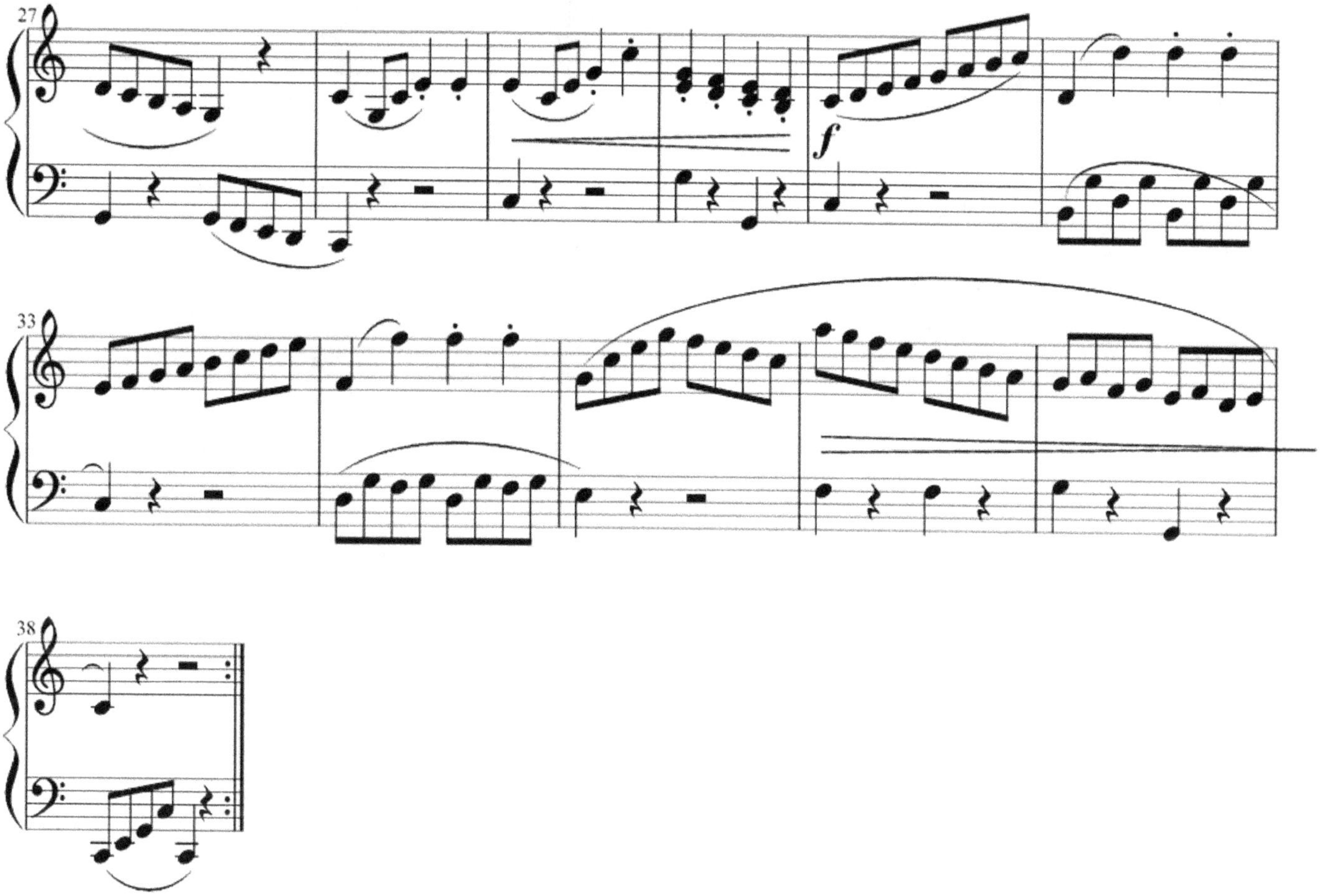
27
f
33
38

Sonatine

Op. 36 No.1, 3

Muzio Clementi

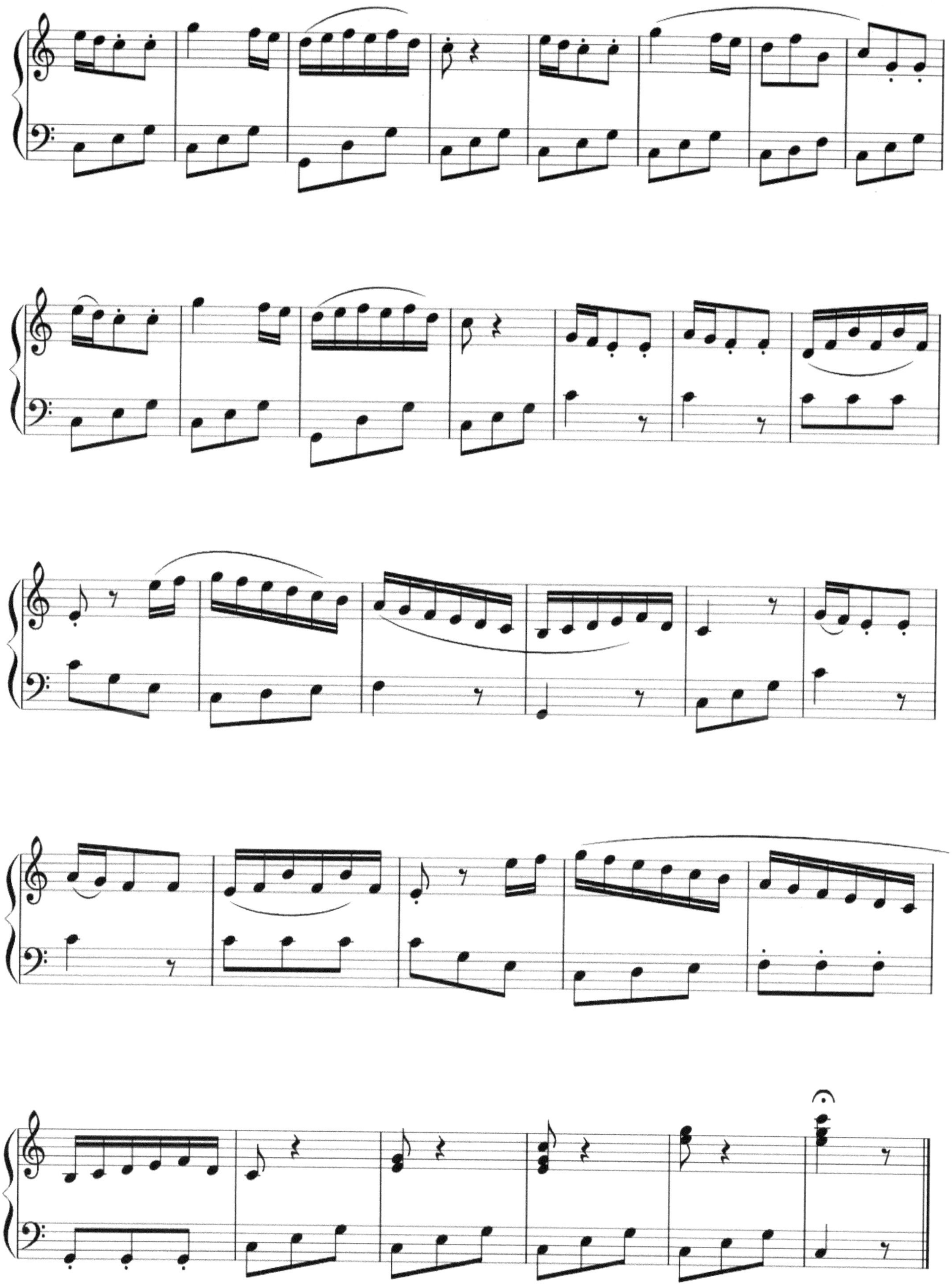